African American History
Civil Rights Movement

By Erinn Banting

Published by Weigl Publishers Inc.
350 5th Avenue, Suite 3304, PMB 6G
New York, NY 10118-0069

Website: www.weigl.com

Library of Congress Cataloging-in-Publication Data available upon request.
Fax 1-866-44-WEIGL for the attention of the Publishing Records department.

ISBN 978-1-59036-882-4 (hard cover)
ISBN 978-1-59036-883-1 (soft cover)

Printed in the United States of America
1 2 3 4 5 6 7 8 9 0   12 11 10 09 08

Weigl acknowledges Getty Images as its primary image supplier for this title.

Editor: Heather C. Hudak
Designer: Terry Paulhus

Contents

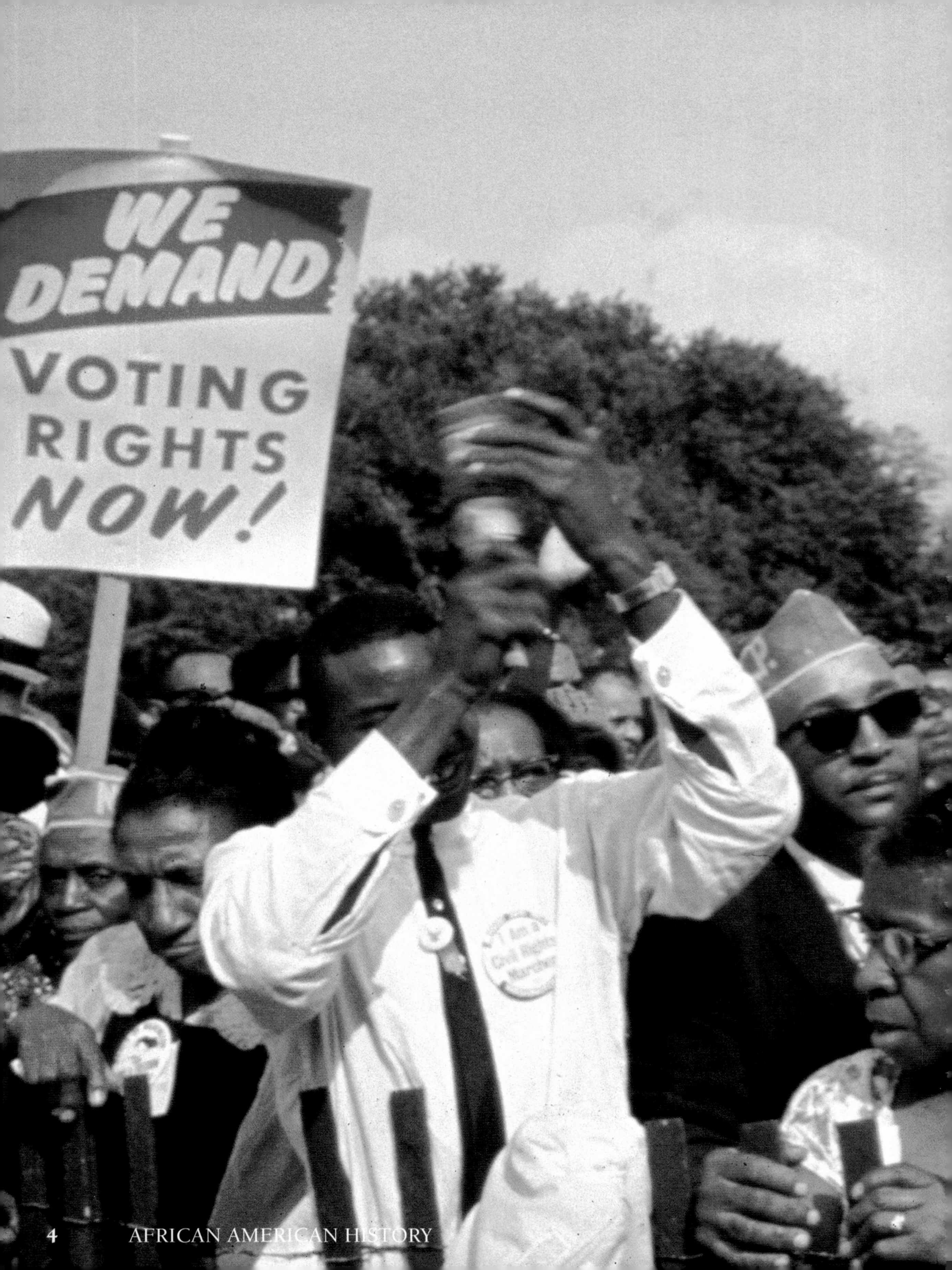
WE DEMAND
VOTING RIGHTS NOW!

A Movement Towards Freedom

Many people have shaped the history of the United States. Among these are the men and women who fought for the **civil rights** of all Americans. Civil rights are the basic rights guaranteed to the **citizens** of a country. These rights include the right to vote, the right to own property, and the right to personal freedom. Personal freedom is a person's right not to be subjected to imprisonment, arrest, or other physical coercion. Civil rights, which are protected by the government, ensure all people have equal opportunities. For hundreds of years in the United States, people were **discriminated** against because of their gender or cultural background. African Americans were among the groups that faced discrimination, **segregation**, and violence.

To fight discrimination and inequality, activists, leaders, and citizens formed the civil rights movement. The men and women who participated in this movement risked their jobs, safety, and lives to ensure that African Americans were guaranteed civil rights. The historic events that formed this movement took place between 1954 and 1968. These events forever changed the history of the United States and did much to change the treatment of the African American people in the country.

Martin Luther King, Jr. was an important figure in the civil rights movement.

TECHNOLOGY LINK
To find out more about the events and people that shaped the civil rights movement, visit **www.pbs.org/wnet/aaworld/timeline/civil_01.html**.

Discrimination and Segregation

The first African slaves were brought to America in 1619. They were kidnapped from their homes in Africa, sent to the Americas by boat and forced to work on farms, called **plantations**, against their will. Slaves were considered the property of their masters and had no rights.

Division and the Civil War

Throughout the 1700s and early 1800s, the number of slaves brought to the United States increased. The southern states relied on agricultural export of the crops they grew on their sprawling plantations. They used slaves to produce the crops.

In the North, **industrialization** changed the **economy**. People began to use machinery to process goods, so slaves were no longer required. This made people question whether it was right to own slaves at all. The slavery debate was one of the issues that sparked the **Civil War**, which raged between the northern and southern United States between 1861 and 1865.

Early Steps

President Abraham Lincoln changed history when his government passed the Emancipation Proclamation in 1862. The proclamation declared that all slaves in the South had to be freed. Then, in 1865, the government declared it illegal to own a slave. Many southern plantation owners refused to follow this law.

New Hope and New Struggles

Some people reacted to the new laws with hatred and violence. **Terrorist** groups, such as the **Ku Klux Klan**, were formed, particularly in the South. Members of the Ku Klux Klan opposed equality and freedom for African Americans. They tortured, beat, and killed hundreds of African Americans and other supporters of equal rights.

Some states, including Ohio, Indiana, Illinois, and South Carolina, passed their own laws to limit the rights of African Americans. The **Jim Crow Laws** restricted African

Americans from using public facilities such as restaurants or transportation. Parks and public washrooms were segregated, which meant they had separate entrances or sections for African Americans.

The Great Migration

Frustrated and fearing for their lives, many African Americans **migrated** north in the early 1900s. Between 1910 and 1920, about two million African Americans moved to cities such as New York, Chicago, and Detroit for better opportunities and jobs. In the North as well, people faced **racism** and discrimination. Many neighborhoods segregated public places, and businesses refused to hire African Americans.

Quick Facts

Segregation worsened in 1896 when the **Supreme Court** ruled that **facilities** could be segregated for African Americans as long as they were provided the same quality of facilities as other Americans.

The National Association of the Advancement of Colored People (NAACP) was formed in 1909 following the **lynching** of two African Americans in Illinois. It is one of the longest-running civil rights groups in the history of the world.

Marcus Garvey, a journalist with a paper called *The Watchman*, began the United Negro Improvement Association (UNIA) in Jamaica in 1914. He believed African Americans should be proud of their **heritage** and promoted better conditions for them. He set up the first branch in the United States in 1917.

Between May and October 1919, a series of violent riots broke out across the United States. The violent period was mainly the result of racism. It was called "Red Summer" as hundreds of people were injured or killed.

Time for Change

World War II changed people's lives around the globe. It had an impact on the civil rights movement in the United States. The factories that built equipment and produced supplies and goods were segregated. To fill the demand for goods, and in response to protests, President Franklin D. Roosevelt declared segregation was not to be part of war industries.

The End of the War and the Committee on Civil Rights
The end of World War II prompted more changes in the United States.

In 1947, President Harry S. Truman organized the Committee on Civil Rights. He was angered by the violence toward African Americans who had risked their lives fighting on behalf of the United States in the war.

President Truman asked the committee to look for ways to change existing laws, or pass new laws, to protect the lives and rights of citizens. The committee recommended ways to end segregation, to stop violent acts such as lynching, and to protect voters' rights.

NAACP Legal Defense Fund

African Americans formed groups to take a stand for equal rights. They wanted to use the few rights they had to change society. In 1909, W.E.B. Du Bois and others formed the National Association for the Advancement of Colored People (NAACP).

The NAACP filed lawsuits to challenge the unfair treatment of African Americans. The result of the rulings in these cases often required that governments or communities to change their laws or practices if they discriminated against African Americans.

In 1940, the NAACP Legal Defense Fund grew from the original organization. To this day, the NAACP Legal Defense Fund supports minority groups that require legal representation. It continues to stand up for the civil rights of all citizens.

W.E.B. Du Bois was one of the founding members of the NAACP.

Brown v. The Board of Education

One of the hundreds of cases filed by the NAACP was *Brown v. The Board of Education of Topeka*. The case was filed by lawyer Thurgood Marshall on behalf of Linda Brown, a 17-year-old student who was not allowed to attend her local high school because she was African American. Instead, she had to travel across town to go to school, even though there was a school just blocks from her home.

At the time, the law stated that schools could be segregated as long as the facilities and education offered were equal. This was not the case. African American students had no supplies, their teachers were not well educated, and the buildings where they attended school were in poor condition.

Linda Brown was not allowed to attend the local high school due to segregation.

Groups, such as the NAACP, believed that a good education was key to freedom and equality. Thurgood Marshall, a lawyer for the NAACP, worked on the *Brown v. Board of Education* case.

A Historic Ruling

In the *Brown v. The Board of Education of Topeka* case, Thurgood Marshall argued that schools had rarely, if ever, been equal. He suggested that this inequality harmed African American children because it damaged their confidence and the way they viewed themselves within their communities. To the delight of the lawyer, the judge who heard the case agreed. In 1954, the Supreme Court finally ruled that segregation in schools was **unconstitutional**. The ruling came as a big relief to African Americans.

The White Citizens Council

As they had done in the past, many southern states opposed the Supreme Court's ruling. Some communities closed their public schools and opened private schools that only students of European ancestry could attend. Some people formed groups, such as The White Citizens Council, that opposed desegregation. Members claimed they used peaceful and lawful methods to protest desegregation. However, the organization was associated with violent incidents against African Americans.

Bravery and Change

Groups such as the NAACP continued to take a stand for equal rights, but most people did not see big changes in their daily lives. Some people felt that the only way to change society was to take action.

They did not want to wait for the government to make improvements.

Rosa's Refusal

One of the most important protests of the civil rights movement began in

In the segregated public transportation system, African Americans were forced to sit in the back of public trains and buses.

Montgomery, Alabama, on December 1, 1955. At the time, many cities and states operated segregated public transportation systems. African Americans were forced to sit in the back of public trains and buses, and in stations, they had separate facilities. Tired of the constant discrimination against African Americans, Rosa Parks refused to give up her seat to a passenger of European ancestry.

The bus driver called the police, and Rosa was arrested and put in jail. People in the local community quickly heard about Rosa's arrest. Rosa was the head of her local NAACP chapter, and the group immediately offered to take on Rosa's case.

Rosa's refusal to give up her seat inspired people in Montgomery and across the United States to take action against injustice and racism. For her contribution to the movement, Rosa is nicknamed the "mother of the civil rights movement."

Who was Rosa Parks?

Rosa Parks was born on February 4, 1913, in Tuskegee, Alabama. Her father, James McCauley, was a carpenter. Her mother, Leona Edwards, was a teacher. When Rosa was young, she and her mother moved to Pine Level, Alabama. At age 11, Rosa was enrolled in the Montgomery Industrial School for Girls. From there, she went to the Alabama State Teacher's College High School.

In 1932, Rosa married Raymond Parks. Rosa and Raymond supported early civil rights protests in the 1930s and became active members of the NAACP in 1943.

Rosa died on October 24, 2005, in her Detroit apartment. She was 92 years old.

Rosa moved to Detroit, Michigan in 1957. There, she worked for the African Methodist Episcopal Church and Congressman John Conyers. She co-founded the Rosa and Raymond Parks Institute for Self Development, which continues to work with young people to teach them how they can make a difference in their lives and the lives of others.

Rosa received many awards and honors during her lifetime, including more than 40 honorary **doctorate degrees** and the Martin Luther King, Jr. Non-violent Peace Prize.

Montgomery Bus Boycott

People wanted to show their support for Rosa Parks. They believed it was time to end segregation in the public transportation system. A group of activists, including a local **minister** named Martin Luther King, Jr., formed a group called the Montgomery Improvement Association (MIA).

The MIA encouraged Montgomery citizens to **boycott** the public transportation system. This had an enormous impact because African American riders bought as many as 40,000 fares a day. Without these fares, bus companies worried they would be put out of business.

Danger and Threats

Bus companies, local government, and many citizens did not support the boycott. They tried to stop the protest. People who organized **carpools**, to help get passengers from place to place, were arrested.

Many African Americans took part in the Montgomery Bus Boycott, which was encouraged by the MIA.

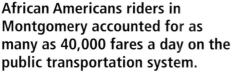

African Americans riders in Montgomery accounted for as many as 40,000 fares a day on the public transportation system.

Boycotters were jailed. Martin Luther King, Jr. received death threats.

Final Success!
In 1956, the Supreme Court ruled that segregation on public transportation was unconstitutional. The boycott and the actions of Rosa Parks inspired others to stand up for their rights, which eventually led to the ruling being in favor of the African Americans.

Quick Facts

The bus boycott lasted a total of 382 days.

During the boycott, a bomb was thrown through the front window of Martin Luther King, Jr.'s home. He and his family were not harmed.

On the day Rosa Parks was arrested, activist and teacher Jo Ann Robinson stayed up all night writing and making 35,000 copies of a pamphlet that encouraged African Americans to participate in the boycott.

AFRICAN AMERICAN HISTORY

Martin Luther King, Jr.

Martin Luther King, Jr., the MIA, and the Montgomery Bus Boycott gained a great deal of attention. King became one of the central members of the civil rights movement, and his teachings inspire people around the world even today.

Early Beginnings

Born in Atlanta, Georgia, in 1929, Martin Luther King, Jr. was raised during one of the most difficult times in history for African Americans.

At age 15, King attended Morehouse College in Atlanta, Georgia. After college, he attended Crozer Theological Seminary in Pennsylvania, where he studied to become a minister. Before accepting a position at the Dexter Avenue Baptist Church, where both his father and grandfather had been ministers, King completed his doctorate degree at Boston University in 1954.

Working for Peace

As a minister and community leader, King had a great influence on the civil rights movement. He was a gifted speaker, and his message of non-violence inspired people to take action. During the Montgomery Bus Boycott, King gained national attention. People of all races and backgrounds viewed him as a hero. This led to increased support for the civil rights movement.

Inspiring Change

At the height of the civil rights movement, between 1957 and 1968, King made more than 2,500 public appearances and traveled more than 6 million miles across the country. He participated in protests and wrote articles and books to educate people about the injustices African Americans faced.

A Lifetime of Achievements

King's work and achievements have inspired thousands of people to make changes in their lives, communities, and countries. During his lifetime, he received five honorary degrees. In 1963, *Time Magazine* named King, Man of the Year, an extraordinary accomplishment for an African American at the time. He was the youngest person to be awarded the Nobel Peace Prize in 1964. King's career came to a halt on April 4, 1968, when he was **assassinated** outside his motel room in Memphis, Tennessee.

Gloria Ray

Terrance Roberts

Melba Pattillo

Elizabeth Eckford

Ernest Green

Minnijean Brown

Jefferson Thomas

Carlotta Walls

Thelma Mothershed

The Little Rock Nine

Three years following the Supreme Court's ruling that banned segregation in public schools, African Americans in the South continued to struggle for equality. In Little Rock, Arkansas, a group of African American students nicknamed "The Little Rock Nine" gained national attention for their efforts to exercise their civil rights.

An Equal Education

In 1957, most businesses and public places in Little Rock were desegregated. Many people of European ancestry were unhappy with desegregation and did not want their children to attend school with African Americans. As a compromise, the community agreed to admit a limited number of African American students to its local high school. Nine African American students were selected to attend Little Rock Central High based on their grades and attendance records.

Turned Away

Members of the community who opposed desegregation planned a protest to prevent the nine African American students from entering the school. Orval Faubus, who was the state governor and known to be in favor of segregation, sent the National Guard to keep out the students. For days, the nine students were barred from the school. A federal judge ordered the governor to admit the students, but he refused.

When a court order forced Faubus to remove the troops from the school on September 23, the African American students were allowed to enter the school through back doors. Protesters broke out in a **riot** and attacked reporters and African Americans.

A Message from the President

President Dwight D. Eisenhower sent federal troops to the Little Rock high school to protect the students and keep the peace on September 25. The Little Rock Nine included Thelma Mothershed, Minnijean Brown, Elizabeth Eckford, Gloria Ray, Jefferson Thomas, Melba Pattillo, Terrence Roberts, Carlotta

Troops turned African American students away from the school.

Walls, and Ernest Green. They were treated poorly by the other students. Minnijean Brown, finished the school year at Central High. Brown finished school in New York. The national attention they received because of their struggles inspired more people to join the fight for civil rights.

Quick Facts

The protest in Little Rock was the first time a president sent **federal** troops to enforce a desegregation law.

At the Arkansas State Capitol, there is a statue of "The Little Rock Nine" called *Testament.*

On November 9, 1999, members of the "The Little Rock Nine" were awarded the Congressional Medal of Honor for their bravery and contribution to the civil rights movement.

Sit-ins

Boycotts and demonstrations inspired African Americans to join the civil rights movements. People began to see that taking action could create change.

Sitting Down for Their Rights

The first "sit-in" took place on February 1, 1960, in North Carolina. Joseph McNeil, Izell Blair, Franklin McCain, and David Richmond, four students from the North Carolina Agricultural and Technical College, sat at a lunch counter reserved for customers of European ancestry. Lunch counters were places in department stores where customers could have a snack or a coffee while they took a break from shopping.

When refused service, the students did not leave. They remained seated until the store closed. The next day, they returned to the store with more students and sat at the counter again.

Sit-ins Spread

News of the sit-in spread, inspiring more people to act. For the first time during the civil rights movement, young people felt empowered to take action. Store owners reacted in many different ways to the protests. Even though the students' acts were nonviolent, some store owners called the police to arrest them for causing disturbance. Customers reacted violently, shoving or burning

Like many public places, lunch counters were segregated for several years.

protesters with cigarettes. Still, the protesters did not get violent.

Some stores closed their lunch counters, but many were forced to desegregate them to avoid losing business. By the end of 1960, more than 80 cities and towns across the country had desegregated counters.

"Jail, No Bail"

"Jail, no **bail**" was a term introduced by a group of students in Rock Hill, South Carolina, in 1961. Robert McCullough, John Gaines, Thomas Gaither, Clarence Graham, W.T. Massey, Willie McCleod, James Wells, David Williamson Jr., and Mack Workman were arrested and jailed for holding a sit-in. They were sentenced to spend 30 days in jail or pay a $100 fine. The group became known as the Friendship Nine because most of the students attended Friendship Junior College.

The group gained attention when they refused to pay a fine or post bail to be released from prison. Civil rights activists thought paying a fine or bail showed that their arrests were just. Serving time in jail gained public attention.

The Student Non-violent Coordinating Committee (SNCC)

The success of sit-ins prompted a group of students from Shaw University in Raleigh, North Carolina, to form a group called the Student Nonviolent Coordinating Committee (SNCC). The group was formed to organize sit-ins and protests across the United States. It worked to bring attention to the civil rights movement and gain the participation of young people in the fight for equality. The group, made up of students of all races, organized and participated in hundreds of protests during the civil rights movement.

Freedom Riders

In 1947, the Supreme Court ruled that it was not legal to segregate vehicles that traveled through more than one state. The Congress of Racial Equality (CORE) wanted to see if the ruling would be followed. To test this, CORE sent 16 men— eight African Americans, and eight of European ancestry—on a two-week trek across Virginia, Kentucky, Tennessee, and North Carolina. Most of the men were arrested on complaints of people who were against African Americans being treated as their equals.

CORE decided to try again in 1961, when the Supreme Court ruled that segregation in interstate travel was unconstitutional. This meant that this type of segregation conflicted with the constitutional right of liberty for all U.S. citizens. It was also unconstitutional to have separate facilities in bus stations.

CORE planned a "Freedom Ride" from Washington, DC, to New Orleans. The ride was similar to the 1947 journey, but included both men and women and used both interstate vehicles and bus terminals.

Resistance for Freedom

When the travelers reached South Carolina, they were met by a mob. The passengers were attacked. Police were called to protect the African American riders who wanted to use the facilities reserved for passengers of European ancestry.

The riders met with even more resistance in Georgia. In Alabama, a group that opposed desegregation surrounded the bus. They broke its windows and slashed its tires. The passengers narrowly escaped when the mob set the bus on fire. Even though their lives were at risk, they boarded another bus and continued their journey.

In Anniston and Birmingham, the riders were beaten. Many were hospitalized. Fearing for their own safety, bus drivers in Birmingham refused to drive the riders any farther. Most of the riders flew to New Orleans to avoid further danger.

Birmingham to New Orleans

CORE thought that ending the ride would show others that protesters could be defeated. The remaining riders, along with the SNCC and the Nashville Student Movement, decided to complete the ride. They wanted to demonstrate that violence would not stop them from pursuing equal rights. At each stop, the group was met with increased violence. President John F. Kennedy ordered the governor of Alabama to protect the protesters. A police

Quick Facts

John Lewis, one of the leaders of the SNCC, participated in the 1961 Freedom Rides. Lewis was first elected to the U.S. House of Representatives in 1987.

The SNCC also called the Freedom Rides a "Journey of Reconciliation."

James Zwerg, a man of European ancestry who participated in the freedom rides, was beaten and nearly killed in Montgomery.

helicopter accompanied the bus to Montgomery, but did not travel farther. Hundreds of people waited to beat the riders, but the riders continued their journey. They did not abandon the ongoing fight for equal civil rights.

The Freedom Riders were provided protection against the mob awaiting them.

The Southern Christian Leadership Conference (SCLC)

In 1957, Martin Luther King, Jr., and a group of fellow ministers founded the Southern Christian Leadership Conference (SCLC). They built on the work of the NAACP, but they believed that change would happen more quickly through peaceful demonstrations.

The SCLC promoted the ideals of Christianity and a well-known spiritual leader in India named Mahatma Gandhi. Gandhi helped to end British rule in India through peaceful protests. King believed Gandhi's success should be an inspiration for civil rights activists.

Challenging Resistance

In the early 1960s, groups such as the SCLC focused on parts of the United States where people had resisted equality and freedom for African Americans. Their first target was Birmingham, Alabama, which was considered the most segregated city in the United States.

On April 3, 1963, Martin Luther King, Jr., Ralph Abernathy, and another founder of the SCLC, Fred Shuttlesworth, began the Birmingham Campaign. The campaign included a series of organized protests, sit-ins, boycotts, and marches. During the campaign, King was arrested and put in jail because he had disobeyed a ban ordering 100 civil rights leaders to abandon their protests.

While King was held in jail, he wrote one of the most influential documents of the civil rights era, "Letter from a Birmingham Jail." In the letter, King urged people to continue non-violent protests, regardless of how violently their opposition reacted.

Reverend Jesse Jackson (left), Ralph Abernathy (center), and Andrew Young (right) were part of the SCLC.

Defying Violence

When King was released from jail, he joined the next protest. On May 2, 1963, the SCLC organized a massive march through Birmingham. More than 1,000 students of all ages joined the march. Many, including children, were arrested.

The arrests did not stop the group from marching again the next day. The police chief, Eugene "Bull" Connor, ordered police to use attack dogs to stop the protest. He also ordered firefighters to turn their powerful fire hoses on the group. Hundreds of people were seriously injured.

Across the country, Americans watched on TV as the events unfolded. Despite the danger, protests continued. On May 10, a group of Birmingham business owners met with the SCLC. They agreed to desegregate their businesses and offer jobs to African Americans.

Eugene "Bull" Connor

During the civil rights movement, leaders emerged who challenged injustice and people's views about the equality of human beings. Some leaders, however, promoted hatred and violence against African Americans. In Birmingham, Theophilius Eugene "Bull" Connor publicly supported segregation and was a member of the Ku Klux Klan. He held a great deal of power in Birmingham. Connor was head of the police and fire departments. He was also the commissioner of public safety, the individual responsible for all emergency services.

Connor's order to attack non-violent protesters during the Birmingham Campaign gained national attention. Despite his efforts to limit the rights of African Americans, the events of 1963 showed Americans and the U.S. government the extent of the situation in the South. Connor's actions prompted President John F. Kennedy and Congress to push the Civil Rights Act of 1964. The act guaranteed equal civil rights for all Americans.

Theophilius Eugene "Bull" Connor (left) opposed the civil rights movement.

The March on Washington

Events such as those in Birmingham convinced many Americans to show support for the civil rights movement. People from different cultures joined protests and spoke out about racism and violence against African Americans. The public demanded that the government put an end to racism and violence.

Philip Randolph organized the massive march in support of the Civil Rights Act.

Kennedy Speaks Out

On June 11, 1963, President Kennedy publicly addressed the citizens of the United States. In a televised speech, he spoke out about the violence in Birmingham. He proposed the Civil Rights Act, which would make it illegal to discriminate against people.

Growing Support

Leaders of the civil rights movement thought Kennedy's speech was a

The March on Washington gained a great deal of attention in print and on television.

major victory. However, the act still had to be passed into law by Congress. A. Philip Randolph, a long-time participant in the civil rights movement, organized a massive march in support of the act.

Randolph spread the word about the planned "March on Washington for Jobs and Freedom." Other leaders and civil rights groups joined the planning. These groups included CORE, SCLC, SNCC, NAACP, the Brotherhood of Sleeping Car Porters, and the National Urban League, which was a community-based movement established in 1910, devoted to empowering African Americans.

People March

On August 28, 1963, more than 250,000 people marched from the Washington Monument to the Lincoln Memorial in Washington, DC. Hundreds of police were present to contain the crowd, but the demonstration was peaceful. Civil rights leaders, such as Martin Luther King, Jr., spoke to the crowds. Musicians, including Bob Dylan and Joan Baez, sang. People who were not able to attend watched the historic event on television.

More than 250,000 people took part in the March on Washington on August 28, 1963.

TECHNOLOGY LINK
To find out more about A. Philip Randolph, visit **www.apri.org**.

After the March on Washington

When the March on Washington ended, a group of civil rights leaders visited President Kennedy at the White House to discuss the Civil Rights Act. According to accounts of the meeting, when the leaders entered the room, Kennedy greeted Martin Luther King by saying, "I have a dream." This was a reference to the historic speech King gave at the march. Kennedy praised the leaders for organizing a powerful and peaceful demonstration.

Challenges to the Bill

The movement and the bill faced more challenges after the march. Racist groups lashed out against the march and its leaders. In Birmingham, violence erupted on September 15, 1963, when an African American church was bombed. Four young girls were killed in the bombing, and more than 20 people were injured.

A group of civil rights leaders, including Martin Luther King, Jr., met President Kennedy to discuss the Civil Rights Act.

The Civil Rights Act was stalled when President Kennedy was assassinated on November 22, 1963. The televised attack sent shock through the United States. It was a blow to the country and a setback for the civil rights movement.

"I Have a Dream"

One of Martin Luther King, Jr.'s best-known contributions to the civil rights movement and the history of the United States was the speech he gave at the March on Washington. In his "I Have a Dream" speech, King called for a future where people of all races lived in harmony. To this day, people listen to and read King's important message. This passage from the speech inspires people to fight for equality and justice to this day.

"Let freedom ring. And when this happens, and when we allow freedom to ring—when we let it ring from every village and every hamlet, from every state and every city, we will be able to speed up that day when all of God's children—black men and white men, Jews and Gentiles, Protestants and Catholics—will be able to join hands and sing in the words of the old Negro spiritual: "Free at last! Free at last! Thank God Almighty, we are free at last!"

Civil Rights Act of 1964

President Kennedy's assassination stalled the passage of the Civil Rights Act of 1964. However, Kennedy's **successor**, Lyndon B. Johnson, saw that the bill became a reality.

Opposition

Not all Americans wanted the Civil Rights Act to be passed. Senator and later governor of South Carolina, James Strom Thurmond, a Republican at the time of the passing of the bill, was so against the bill that he threw his shoe at a senator who supported it.

An Important Decision

Despite opposition, the Civil Rights Act was passed. Johnson signed the act into effect on July 2, 1964. The act made it illegal to discriminate against a person because of his or her race. All public places had to be desegregated, including restaurants, theaters, and washrooms in the cities. In addition, any state that did

The Civil Rights Act was signed on July 2, 1964.

not comply with the act could be denied funding from the federal government. School boards that did not guarantee education for all students were also denied funding.

The passing of the Civil Rights Act was an important step in the civil rights movement. However, many African Americans continued to face violence, mistreatment, and were denied their rights.

Trouble in Mississippi

Mississippi was widely known as the most segregated state in America. The state earned this reputation because of several high profile events that involved terror and violence against African Americans in the 1950s and 1960s. One of these cases involved the beating and murder of a 14-year-old boy named Emmett Till.

Till had been spending the summer with his uncle, Moses Wright, in Money, Mississippi. In August 1955, he went to visit other family in Delta, Mississippi. On August 24, Till went to Bryant's Grocery Store and Meat Market for snacks. The storeowner, Carolyn Bryant, claimed Till said something inappropriate to her. Three days later, Bryant's husband Roy and his brother J.W. Milam kidnapped Till from his cousins' home. They beat and shot Till, and dumped his body in the Tallahatchie River. When

Till's body was discovered, the police and members of the community tried to hide the murder. Less than a month after Till was killed, the brothers appeared in court, but they were acquitted on September 23, 1955.

The civil rights movement witnessed scenes of violence against people who supported equality. Some people and groups used violence to scare people into giving up the fight for equal rights. Many leaders of the civil rights movement were assassinated. The assassinations of leaders, such as Martin Luther King, Jr. and Malcolm X, created fear and confusion amongst African American people. However, they did not give up the fight for equal rights, even though their lives and security were threatened.

Till and his friends went to Bryant's Grocery store in Mississippi on August 24, 1955.

Freedom Summer

The Right to Vote

In 1962, the Council of Federated Organizations (COFO) was formed. COFO wanted to bring all civil rights groups together to ensure they were working toward a common goal. COFO organized an event called Freedom Vote. At the event, organizers conducted a **mock election**. African Americans who were not registered to vote were invited to participate. The mock vote pitted the actual candidates against candidates from the interracial Freedom Party. This gave voters the opportunity to show support for actual candidates or those from the newly formed Mississippi Freedom Democratic Party (MFDP), which was organized to fight for African American representation in the Democratic Party.

More than 90,000 people voted in the mock election. This helped in curbing, to some extent, African Americans' mortal fear of the consequences of showing up to vote in Mississippi. After the election, they felt confident that their votes were wanted by the candidates.

The Election of 1964

The success of the Freedom Vote excited COFO. Following this project, COFO organized a drive that was nicknamed Freedom Summer. In 1964, members worked to register African Americans to vote in the upcoming federal election. Students came to Mississippi from around the country to help. They set up education programs to teach African Americans about their rights, the voting process, and African American history. This was a registration drive that made the African Americans confident to vote.

Violence and Opposition

Groups, such as the Ku Klux Klan, lashed out at African Americans and others supporting the movement. In June 1964, three civil rights activists, named Michael Schwerner, Andrew Goodman, and James Chaney, disappeared. Their bodies were not discovered until August 4. They had been shot, and James Chaney, who was the only African American of the three, had also been badly beaten.

The 1964 Democratic Convention

In June, the names of four MFDP candidates were on the Democratic primary ballot as **delegates** to be sent to the Democratic National Convention in Atlantic City. The presence of African Americans in the Democratic Party divided the 1964 Democratic Convention. When delegates from the MFDP insisted on participating, many Democrats turned their backs on their own party. MFDP delegates were not recognized by the Democratic Party and challenged that decision. The

ANDREW GOODMAN   JAMES EARL CHANEY   MICHAEL HENRY SCHWERNER

RACE:	White	Negro	White
SEX:	Male	Male	Male
DOB:	November 23, 1943	May 30, 1943	November 6, 1939
POB:	New York City	Meridian, Mississippi	New York City
AGE:	20 years	21 years	24 years
HEIGHT:	5'10"	5'7"	5'9" to 5'10"
WEIGHT:	150 pounds	135 to 140 pounds	170 to 180 pounds
HAIR:	Dark brown; wavy	Black	Brown
EYES:	Brown	Brown	Light blue
TEETH:		Good: none missing	
SCARS AND MARKS:		1 inch cut scar 2 inches above left ear.	Pock mark center of forehead, slight scar on bridge of nose, appendectomy scar, broken leg scar.

SHOULD YOU HAVE OR IN THE FUTURE RECEIVE ANY INFORMATION CONCERNING THE WHEREABOUTS OF THESE INDIVIDUALS, YOU ARE REQUESTED TO NOTIFY ME OR THE NEAREST OFFICE OF THE FBI.

Posters were circulated for the three missing civil rights activists.

Democratic Party agreed to allow two MFDP delegates to participate without voting rights. The MFDP refused this offer, but it continued to fight for representation in its state government.

Quick Facts

James Meredith was the first African American student to attend the University of Mississippi. Resistance was so great that President Kennedy sent troops to protect him until his graduation.

In the early 1960s, only five percent of African Americans in Mississippi were registered to vote. Most were afraid that they would face a threat to their life if they tried to vote or register to vote.

The education programs set up by COFO were called "Freedom Schools."

Montgomery March

The fight for the right to vote did not end in Mississippi. Freedom Summer had taught people, through mock voting, the importance of exercising their rights. By 1964, the number of registered African American voters jumped from 5 percent to 42 percent.

Stopping the Vote

Voter registration was on the rise, but many people were afraid to vote. Racist governments enforced strict and impossible rules for African American voters. Some were required to pay a tax. Most African American workers earned much lower wages than people from other backgrounds, so they could not afford to pay the fee. Some communities required African Americans to pass a written test before they could vote. Many had difficulty with reading or writing because they had received little or no education. In addition, their lives and safety were threatened if they exercised their right to vote.

The Selma Campaign

Selma, Alabama, was one of the most troubled cities in the South. Open racism by the city's leaders, including Governor George Wallace and the

Children watched as protesters marched to the state capital during the Montgomery March.

city's sheriff, encouraged people to prevent African Americans from exercising their rights. By 1965, only two percent of the 150,000 eligible African American voters in Selma were registered to vote.

In response, the SCLC organized the Selma Campaign. Hundreds of protesters gathered. Led by Martin Luther King, Jr., the protesters marched through Selma's streets to the courthouse. Most were arrested and jailed.

Triumphs and Tragedies

Many people across the country were alarmed by the violence in Selma. The SCLC responded by organizing a highly publicized march from Selma to Montgomery so they could speak to Governor Wallace about the ongoing violence against African Americans in his state.

The March to Montgomery

The protesters who gathered for the Montgomery March set out on March 7, 1964. They were stopped at the Edmund Pettus Bridge, only six blocks into their journey. Police and state troopers used clubs and **tear gas** to

By the time the march ended in Montgomery, there were more than 250,000 participants.

Quick Facts

The first march to Montgomery was later called "Bloody Sunday" because about 500 protesters were injured.

About 600 protesters joined Martin Luther King, Jr. for the third march on March 21.

force them to return to Selma. The violence did not stop the protesters from marching again on March 21st. This time, they were joined by other supporters who had seen the beatings and attacks on television. The federal guard was sent to help protect the people in the march and enforce their right to hold the demonstration.

The Voting Rights Act of 1965

African Americans were eager to vote, lining up at poll stations.

Campaigns launched by the SCLC to promote voter registration drew attention to the fact that African Americans still struggled for equality in the South. In 1965, President Johnson proposed the Voting Rights Act, which guaranteed the right to vote to all Americans.

The Act
In many southern states, governments did not protect or guarantee the rights of African Americans to vote. The act was created to give the federal government more control over the enforcement of voting rights. Tests were outlawed, and state governments had to request approval for all voting policies before they put them in place. The act took power and jobs away from state officials, many of whom were known racists.

Black Power

Non-violent groups and leaders within the civil rights movement had achieved major change. Some African Americans were frustrated that they had suffered hundreds of years of mistreatment, racism, and violence. They did not think non-violence was the answer.

The March Against Fear

In June 1966, James Meredith organized the March Against Fear. Meredith was the first African American to attend the University of Mississippi. He was a well-known activist in the civil rights movement. On his way from Memphis to Jackson, Tennessee, Meredith was shot. This act of violence angered many activists. Days later, a group that included Martin Luther King, Jr. from the SCLC and Floyd McKissick and Stokley Carmichael from the SNCC gathered in Memphis to continue Meredith's march.

At a rally on June 16, 1966, Carmichael gave a speech in which he called for African Americans to exercise their "Black Power" in response to racism. The term spawned a movement. Different groups formed, many

of which promoted violence and the separation of African communities. It also encouraged people to promote and feel pride for their African heritage.

African Americans took pride in their heritage, using "Black Power" as a platform against racism.

Malcolm X

Non-violence was opposed well before the 1960s. One leader who disagreed with non-violence was Malcolm X. Born Malcolm Little, he changed his last name to X to protest the fact that, when many Africans were brought to America, they were not permitted to keep their last names. The X also represented the mark many slave owners burned into their slaves' arms to identify them.

Between 1946 and 1952, Malcolm served time in prison for robbery. While, there he joined the Nation of **Islam**. This group promoted both traditional Islamic beliefs as well as **nationalism** for African Americans. Upon his release from prison, Malcolm became a major figure in the Nation of Islam. Under his guidance, membership in the Nation of Islam quickly increased. Malcolm rose up the ranks, becoming the

Malcolm X was a major figure in the Nation of Islam.

second-highest leader in the movement, next to Elijah Muhammad. Throughout the civil rights movement, Malcolm preached in Harlem and spoke at universities. His message that African Americans should demand equal rights "by any means necessary" earned him the nickname "Father of the Black Power Movement." He did not believe in integration and was critical of African Americans' interest in key events, such as the March on Washington.

In 1963, Elijah and Malcolm began to differ in their views on the Nation of Islam. Their relationship came to an end when Elijah ordered Malcolm to observe a period of silence after Malcolm publicly stated his opinion about the assassination of John F. Kennedy. In 1964, Malcolm left the Nation of Islam.

Over the next few years, Malcolm adopted new ideals. On his pilgrimage to Mecca, Saudi Arabia, he viewed Muslims of different races interacting as equals. This prompted him to think that Islam could transcend racial divides. However, tensions continued to rise between Malcolm and the Nation of Islam. Malcolm received regular death threats, and his family faced constant danger. On February 21, 1965, Malcolm was assassinated while giving a speech at Audubon Ballroom in Harlem. He was shot 16 times by three men who were members of the Nation of Islam.

Organization of Afro-American Unity

In 1964, Malcolm X traveled to Africa. While there, he learned about the Organization of African Unity (OAU). When he returned to New York, he and a writer and activist named John Henrik Clark formed the Organization of Afro-American Unity (OAAU). The organization's goal was to unite African people around the world. The group promoted the complete

separation of African American communities from the rest of the United States.

The group lost support after Malcolm X's assassination and was eventually dissolved.

A New Hope

Participants in the civil rights movement continued to fight for equality through the 1960s. Many **historians** believe that the movement came to an end in 1968, when Martin Luther King, Jr. was assassinated outside his motel room in Memphis, Tennessee. King had traveled to Tennessee in support of a sanitation workers' strike. On April 4th, while standing on the hotel balcony, King was struck by a sniper's shot. Shocked by the violent act toward a peaceful leader, people rioted across the United States. Nearly one year later, on March 10, 1969, James Earl Ray pleaded guilty to King's murder. He was sentenced to 99 years in prison. Later, Ray claimed that he was innocent. He was awaiting a new trial when he died on April 23, 1998.

Condoleezza Rice is the first African American woman to serve as Secretary of State in the United States.

Leading Change

King's death had an impact on the way in which civil rights activists fought for change. Many viewed King as the person who united the movement. Even after his death, people continued to fight for equality and justice for all African Americans.

The achievements of the civil rights movement opened many doors for African Americans. They pursued higher education and worked to get better jobs. They became teachers, doctors, lawyers, and politicians. In Cleveland, Ohio, in 1967, Carl Stokes made history when he became the first African American mayor.

Improvements in economic equality meant that African Americans were paid more fairly. For many years, African American professionals made less money for the same jobs. The federal and state governments continued to push for the full desegregation of schools in the 1960 and 1970s.

The Fight for Change Continues

Through the 1980s, 1990s, and today, many African Americans have worked toward equality and freedom for themselves and people of all races. These people are celebrated in many ways. In 1986, the United States government honored Martin Luther King, Jr. by making his birthday a national holiday.

In entertainment, politics, and the arts, African Americans continue to break barriers. General Colin L. Powell was made the chair of the Joint Chiefs of Staff of the U.S. Military in 1989. In 2001, he became the first African American Secretary of State. Entertainers, such as Oprah Winfrey, have used their profile to educate others about the lives and struggles of people in the United States and around the world. In addition to her television show, Oprah works as an activist in Africa to improve the lives of children and people there. In 2008, Barack Obama became the first African American chosen to run for the president of the United States.

Halle Barry was the first African American to receive an Oscar in the Best Actress category, while Denzel Washington won for Best Actor.

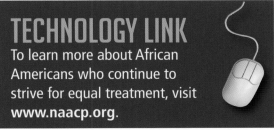

TECHNOLOGY LINK
To learn more about African Americans who continue to strive for equal treatment, visit **www.naacp.org**.

Timeline

1619: Africans are captured and brought to Jamestown, Virginia, to work as slaves.

1619

1807: Congress declares it illegal to bring slaves into the United States.

1831-1861: About 75,000 slaves escape by the Underground Railroad, a network that helped protect and hide escaped slaves so they could find freedom.

1861: The Civil War begins. One of the main issues behind the conflict is to determine if slavery should be allowed.

1909

1863: President Abraham Lincoln passes the Emancipation Proclamation, which legally frees all slaves.

1865: Congress passes the Thirteenth Amendment, which outlaws slavery.

1866: Congress passes the Civil Rights Act, which declares African Americans as citizens.

1881: The first Jim Crow Law is passed in Tennessee.

1896: In Plessy v. Ferguson, the Supreme Court rules that public places may be segregated as long as equal facilities are given to African Americans.

1909: The National Association for the Advancement of Colored People (NAACP) is formed.

1910-1920: During a period known as the Great Migration, about 500,000 African Americans move to northern states.

1861

1914: Marcus Garvey forms the Universal Negro Improvement Association in Jamaica. The group eventually opens branches in the United States.

1919: A series of violent events occur in response to the Great Migration. The period is known as "Red Summer" because of the hundreds of deaths that resulted from the violence.

1600   **1800**   **1850**   **1900**

1942: The Congress of Racial Equality (CORE) is started in Chicago.

1948: President Truman desegregates the army.

1954: In Brown v. Board of Education of Topeka, the Supreme Court rules against school segregation.

1955: The Montgomery Bus Boycott begins when Rosa Parks refuses to give up her seat to a passenger of European ancestry.

1957: A community in Little Rock, Arkansas, opposes desegregation and plans a protest to prevent nine African American students from entering a school that was formerly only for students of European ancestry. The African American students are later called "The Little Rock Nine."

1960: At a Woolworth's lunch counter in Greensboro, North Carolina, four African American college students hold the first sit-in.

1961: The Congress of Racial Equality (CORE) begins to organize Freedom Rides.

1963

1963: Martin Luther King, Jr. writes "Letter from a Birmingham Jail."

1964: Martin Luther King, Jr. is awarded the Nobel Peace Prize.

1965: Malcolm X is assassinated in New York.

1983: Astronaut Guion "Guy" S. Bluford, Jr. becomes the first African American in space, flying aboard the space shuttle *Challenger*.

1985: Philadelphia State Police bomb a house in Philadelphia occupied by an African American activist organization, MOVE, killing 11 occupants and triggering a fire that destroyed a neighborhood and left more than 300 people homeless.

1986: Martin Luther King, Jr.'s birthday is made into a national holiday.

1989: General Colin L. Powell is the first African American to be named chair of the Joint Chiefs of Staff of the U.S. military.

1989: Oprah Winfrey becomes the first African American woman to host a nationally syndicated talk show.

2008: Barack Obama, a politician from Chicago's South Side, becomes the first African American to secure a major party nomination as a presidential candidate.

1961

2008

1950   **1960**   **1980**   **2000**

Activity

What Makes a Leader?

A leader is a person that others can look to as a role model. Leaders have shaped the world we live in. They have changed politics, music, art, and history. In this activity, you will examine what makes a leader.

You will need:

✓ a pen
✓ paper
✓ a dictionary
✓ access to the Internet

First, define the word "leader" in your own words. What are some of the characteristics that leaders have?

Next, look up the word "leader" in the dictionary. Compare that definition to your own. What are some of the traits that you missed or included on your list compared to the dictionary?

Now, think about who your personal leaders are. They could be a parent, a grandparent, a teacher, or a celebrity, for example. Write a short paragraph about this leader and why you look up to this person.

Finally, consider some of the great leaders of the civil rights movement. Choose one, and write a short biography of his or her life. What was his or her impact and what made him or her a great leader?

Test Your Knowledge

Q Who was nicknamed "the mother of the civil rights movement"?

A Rosa Parks

Q Which historic laws were passed in 1964 and 1965?

A The Civil Rights Act of 1964 and the Voting Rights Act of 1965

Q What does NAACP stand for?

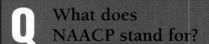

A The National Association for the Advancement of Colored People

Q Which prize did Martin Luther King, Jr. win in 1964?

A The Nobel Peace Prize

Q When did the Supreme court rule against segregation on public transport?

A In 1956

Q How many people attended the March on Washington? What was the name of the famous speech Martin Luther King, Jr. gave at the march?

A 250,000 people attended; "I Have a Dream"

Books

Learn more about the leaders of the civil rights movement by reading the following books.

Woog, Adam. *The Fight Renewed: The Civil Rights Movement*. Thompson Gale, 2006.

Thatcher, Murcia. Rebecca. *The Civil Rights Movement*. Mitchell Lane Publishers Inc. 2005.

Websites

To learn more about African American History and Culture, visit **www.pbs.org/wnet/aaworld/index.html**.

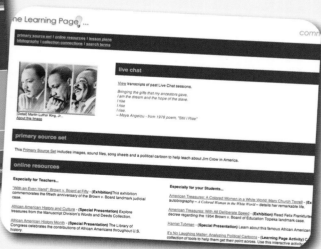

Find out more about the events and the people of the civil rights movement at **http://memory.loc.gov/learn/community/cc_civilrights.php**.

Glossary

assassinated: murdered for political reasons

bail: a fine paid to temporarily release a person from jail

boycott: to protest by refusing to use a public service, or purchase goods and services

carpools: groups of people traveling to work in the same car

citizens: members of a country or political community

civil rights: the basic rights guaranteed to the citizens of a country, such as the right to vote, the right to assembly, and the right to freedom

Civil War: a war fought in the United States between 1861 and 1865; the northern states, which remained in the Union, battled against the southern states, which separated and formed the Confederacy

delegates: representatives at a conference or convention

discriminated: treated a person unfairly because of his or her race, gender, age, or physical or mental condition

doctorate degrees: the highest degrees awarded by a college or university

economy: activities related with the production, distribution, exchange, and consumption of goods and services

facilities: buildings and public places

federal: the central branch of government

heritage: a person's cultural or historical background

historians: people who study history

industrialization: the move from an economy that depends on agriculture to one that depends on the production of goods

Islam: a religion that was founded by an Arab religious leader named Muhammad

Jim Crow Laws: laws that supported segregation in the southern states

Ku Klux Klan: a terrorist group that uses violence against minority groups

lynching: publically torturing and hanging an innocent person

migrated: moved from one location to another

minister: a leader in the Christian church

mock election: an imitation of a real election

nationalism: being devoted to the independence of one's own nation

plantations: large farms that grew crops such as cotton, sugar, tobacco, or coffee

racism: hatred or intolerance of another race

riot: a public act of violence

segregation: separation because of race, gender, or religion

successor: a person who takes over for another in an office or position

Supreme Court: the highest court of the United States

tear gas: a gas that makes the eyes sting but does not damage them; used in dispersing crowds

terrorist: a person who uses extreme acts to frighten others

unconstitutional: against the U.S. Constitution, which sets out the rights and freedoms of all Americans

World War II: a global conflict fought between 1939 and 1945

Index